50 GEMS

Jersey

ANDREW POWELL-THOMAS

AMBERLEY

In memory of Sandie Sewell

First published 2024

Amberley Publishing
The Hill, Stroud
Gloucestershire, GL5 4EP

www.amberley-books.com

British Library Cataloguing in Publication Data.
A catalogue record for this book is available from the British Library.

ISBN 978 1 3981 1285 8 (paperback)
ISBN 978 1 3981 1286 5 (ebook)

Typesetting by SJmagic DESIGN SERVICES, India.
Printed in Great Britain.

Contents

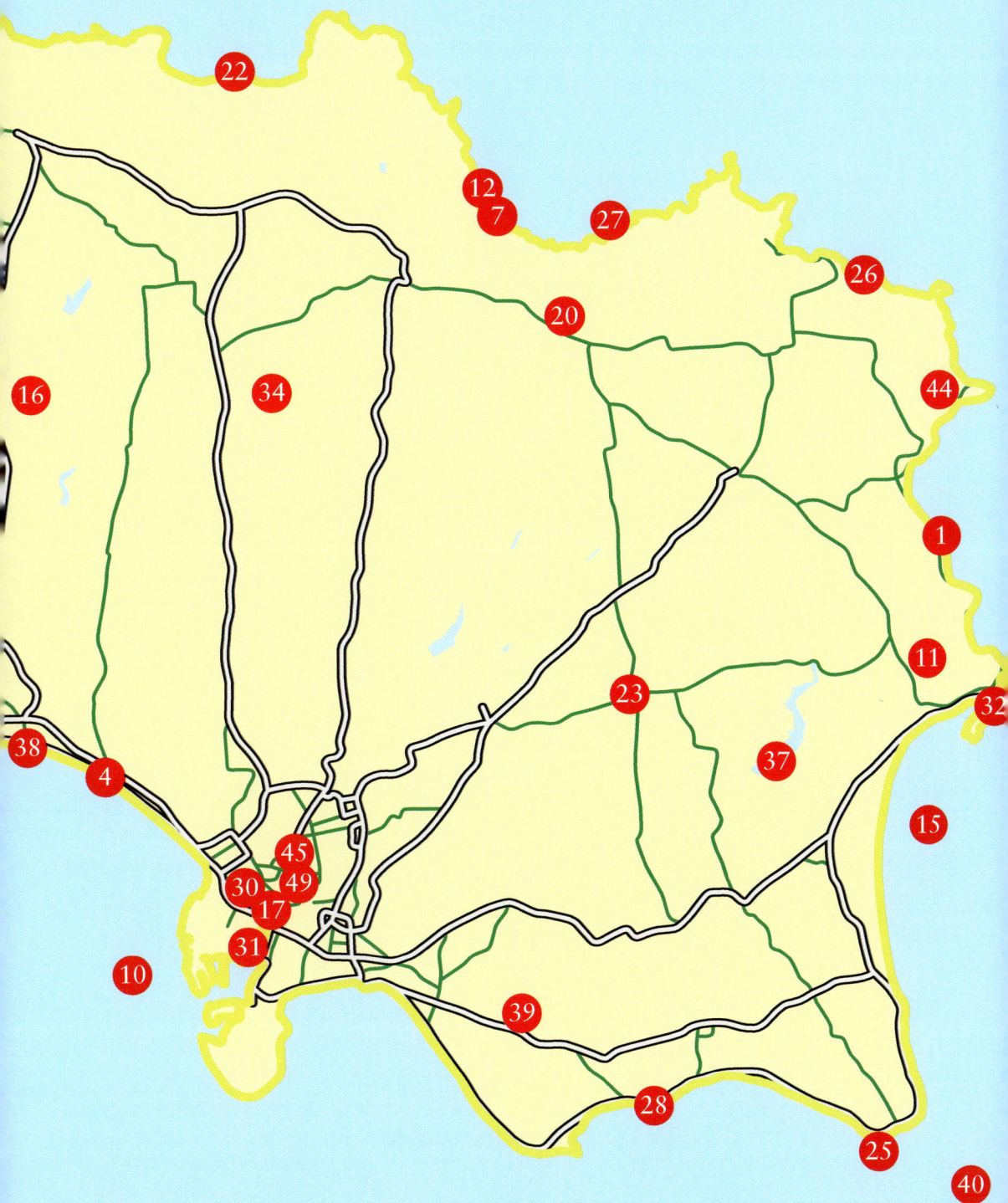

Introduction

Jersey, the largest of the Channel Islands, sits nestled in the English Channel just 12 miles west of the Cotentin peninsula of France. Nearly 100,000 people call this 45-square mile island home, and this small British Crown Dependency understandably mixes the best of British and French cultures. Its sheltered position in the Bay of St Malo means that it is generally warmer and has more sunshine hours than you would get on mainland Britain. Jersey offers an extraordinary variety of landscapes: from beautiful beaches that stretch as far as the eye can see to coastal paths that wind their way over headlands and around dramatic clifftops. There are charming villages around every corner, with open fields and rugged coastline only ever a few miles away, and the remnants of prehistoric humans can be found at a number of Neolithic sites on the island. Due to the island's geographic location, it isn't surprising that there are numerous forts and grand castles dotted all around, as Britain and France tussled over ownership; and the German occupation during the Second World War has left a more recent and permanent mark on the island, with bunkers and command posts easily visible. Condensing so much history, heritage and natural splendour into just fifty gems has been a challenge, and I have endeavoured to include a range of gems that will appeal to everyone, young and old, active and relaxing. Jersey really does have something for everyone.

1. Archirondel Tower and Beach

We begin our tour of Jersey in the east of the island, where the rocky St Catherine's beach and its multitude of small coves are protected by a nineteenth-century built breakwater. Originally, there were two planned, at the northern and southern ends of the beach, which would have created a harbour for the English fleet. However, only the northern arm was completed, and it provides a long promenade that gives some excellent views – on a clear day it is possible to see France from here. Jutting out from the middle of St Catherine's Bay, on an offshore rock called La Roche Rondel, is Archirondel Tower. Taking two years to construct, it was completed in 1794 as tower number 22 of 30 planned around the island by General Conway in order to deter a potential French invasion. Garrisoned with soldiers of the Artillery and Engineers, it was soon decided to add to the position by building a permanent gun platform around the base of the tower. The tower remained part of Jersey's defensive network, and it was garrisoned and operational until the 1860s, when the decision was made to make it redundant. In 1923, the tower was purchased from the Crown by the States of Jersey, although it remained unused and obsolete. However, in the Second World War, German Occupying Forces saw an opportunity to use this already standing defensive position for themselves. The old decrepit floors were replaced with modern concrete ones and a new entrance to the tower was created, along with a small extension for machine guns to be mounted. After the war it once again remained closed, but in 2006 it became registered as owned by the Public of the Island of Jersey, and since 2019, Jersey Heritage have overseen a refit and modernisation of its interior, to enable the tower to be let out as a rather spectacular self-catering property. It is linked to the shoreline by the initial section of the southern arm of St Catherine's Breakwater and offers genuine uninterrupted views of the surrounding area from its roof terrace, which must allow the visitor to capture the most stunning sunsets!

Archirondel Tower is built on the small La Roche Rondel, which was originally a tidal island. (Author's collection)

Archirondel Tower is one of twenty-three towers built on the island by the former Governor of Jersey, Field Marshall Henry Conway. (Author's collection)

2. Batterie Lothringen

The German occupation of Jersey during the Second World War has understandably left its mark on the island. Hitler's plans for Jersey included constructing nine coastal batteries that would cover the gulf of St Malo and offer protection to German shipping between the strategic ports of Brest and Cherbourg on mainland France. These captured ports were vital in allowing the German fleet easy access into the

English Channel and the Atlantic Ocean. Batterie Lothringen was one of these. The location of Noirmont Point was an obvious place to put a defensive coastal battery, jutting out as it does from the south coast of Jersey and offering significant protection to the port of St Helier. Although occupied from the summer of 1940, construction here didn't begin until the spring of 1941 – with three old naval guns from the First World War being installed as a temporary measure whilst work took place on the more permanent concrete positions of the site. The plan was for these positions to house more modern turreted naval guns, but the allied bombing of factories and production lines in Germany meant that the temporary older guns actually became the permanent feature here. As with all large coastal batteries, the site was defended with a number of additional installations such as anti-aircraft guns, heavy machine gun nests, flamethrower positions, pillboxes and a searchlight – not to mention ammunition bunkers, metre upon metre of barbed wire and mine fields. The temporary command post that was built in 1941 was eventually replaced in 1944 with a bigger and stronger command post on the most southerly point of the battery and it looks very much like the bridge of a battleship. This two-storey command post, which was the nerve centre of the site, took a year to construct and is predominately hidden underground – with only the range-finder turret being above ground.

Manned by over 170 men of Naval Artillery Battalion 604, Lothringen was the third battery under their control in the Channel Islands, with the other two on Guernsey and Alderney respectively. Although there were wooden barrack huts on site, the vast majority of the men were actually billeted at the (former) Portelet Holiday Camp. Aside from live firing drills, the guns at Lothringen were only actually fired in anger a few times. In December 1942, its weapons brought down two RAF aircraft that were attacking a German convoy, but the general lack of action was down to the allies understandably steering clear of the area if they could. In the months after D-Day there was an understandable increase in activity around the nearby Cherbourg peninsula, but by the September of 1944, when the allies had liberated the nearby French coastline, they were simply able to avoid Lothringen's guns – making them just an interested spectator to the ongoing liberation of Europe.

When the Channel Islands were finally liberated in May 1945, the large guns were dumped over the cliffs at Les Landes in the north-west of the island, and anything that could be taken from the bunkers was. The Noirmont headland was purchased by the States of Jersey in January 1947 for the public as the island's war memorial and the various bunkers were then sealed up from the public in 1948. They lay there abandoned for over thirty years, until the Channel Islands Occupation Society (CIOS) obtained permission to restore the command bunker and observation tower because of the historical significance of the site – and what a job they have done! Although the external parts of Lothringen, such as the raised concrete gun platforms, are available to see all year round, it is worth keeping an eye out for the days, and there are always a number of these across the year, when the CIOS open up the command bunker – it is staggering. The inside has been lovingly restored to what it would have looked like during the occupation, with the crews' quarters, communications room and the all-important range finder room immaculately presented. Also part of the Noirmont Point site, is the impressive MP1 Naval Direction and Range-Finding Tower. Standing at over 15 metres tall, it was built down into the cliff and is unique on the island as its entrance is on the top floor! Although sealed up and not open to the public, you are able to walk onto the roof to get a splendid view of the coastline.

Above: A view of No. 1 Gun position during the occupation. (Courtesy of the Channel Islands Occupation Society (Jersey))

Below: No. 1 Gun position today. (Author's collection)

Batterie Lothringen during the Second World War, complete with camouflage netting! (Courtesy of the Channel Islands Occupation Society (Jersey))

A close-up of one of the camouflaged 6.5-ton gun barrels during the conflict. (Courtesy of the Channel Islands Occupation Society (Jersey))

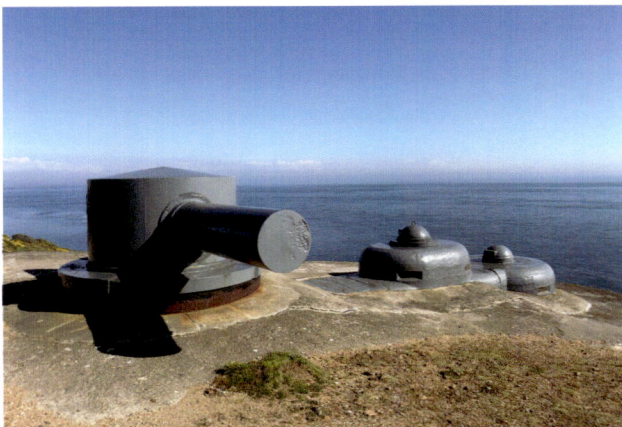

The visible part of the command bunker, or Leitstand, above ground looks like the bridge of a battleship. To the left is the armoured range-finder turret. (Author's collection)

Inside the command bunker are numerous displays and artefacts from the occupation. (Author's collection)

3. Batterie Moltke

Batterie Moltke was another of Hitler's planned nine coastal batteries in Jersey during the Second World War. Foreign workers from the Organisation Todt (OT) were brought across from mainland Europe to the north-west corner of the island at the Les Landes headland, where they stayed in a workers' camp whilst constructing the site that we can still see today. The first big guns arrived in March 1941, and even though the original plan was for the navy to man all of the coastal artillery batteries, it was the army who actually took possession of this site in May 1941, with further guns being transferred here in July 1941. In the summer of 1942, a series of modernisations took place to allow the battery to have more modern turreted naval guns and these emplacements, No. 1 to 4 gun positions, were built over the next ten months – with No. 4 Gun position being the last completed in April 1943. These four emplacements, with their 80-cm-thick concrete floors, are identical in their design. Each position had various ammunition elevators, gun crew access points, shell storage areas, drainage pumps and a seemingly endless length of underground passageways. Although these gun positions are the main focal point of the battery, there were numerous other associated buildings constructed. Large personnel bunkers, each accommodating up to twenty-seven men, were 'attached' to each gun position, along with reserve ammunition bunkers and yet more interconnecting underground tunnels. Add to that anti-aircraft positions, anti-tank and heavy machine gun emplacements, machine gun nests and fixed flamethrower positions, a powerful coastal artillery searchlight and the Coastal Artillery Range-Finding Position M2a, and you have a truly massive site. Further along the coast, there lies a Naval Direction and Range-Finding Tower (MP3) that was built in 1943. Its aim was to control and direct the fire from the coastal batteries by working in unison with the other eight Range-Finding Towers that had been planned for Jersey – although only three were actually completed.

The 5th Battery Army Coastal Artillery Regiment 1265 were responsible for the daily operations at Moltke, with around 100 men stationed here at its peak. Despite the vast number of resources put into the site, Moltke saw very limited action outside of its live firing exercises. The allies knew full well the capabilities of the battery and simply avoided getting into close proximity with it. In one way, it meant that sea around this part of Jersey was indeed under German control, but certainly as the war went on, the large number of troops here were simply being bypassed and became largely a redundant part of the war. In the days and months after D-Day, the battery did engage with Allied shipping, laying down heavy fire on a number of occasions. When Jersey was liberated on 9 May 1945, the men stationed here were taken as prisoners of war, and the liberating forces removed the large guns and simply threw them over the cliffs. Anything that could be reused from the myriad of bunkers and emplacements was taken, and the site was left open for mother nature to reclaim. In the years that followed, the area became a dumping ground for all sorts of things and, ultimately, the gun emplacements were filled in and buried.

In 1978, the Channel Islands Occupation Society (CIOS) were made custodians of No. 4 Gun position and have done a sterling job in the years that have followed in excavating and preserving this part of the site. The footprint of Batterie Moltke covers a great swathe of land and is freely accessible to everyone throughout the year. It is possible to explore several concrete structures that are scattered above ground, whilst the other three main gun emplacements remain completely buried having been infilled after the conflict ended, apart from their concrete gun platforms which lie on the surface. However, No. 4 Gun position has been cleaned out and is regularly opened by CIOS members, and it offers a tantalising glimpse into the engineering that built this site and what daily life would have been like here for German forces during the Second World War. Crews' quarters, ventilation machinery and what seems like miles of tunnels have been restored – with the footprints of those who laid the concrete incredibly still visible on the way out of one! There are numerous artefacts on display: from searchlights, helmets and ordinance to personal items of not just the German troops stationed here, but also aid packages received by the local population.

Above: The army artillery emplacement at No. 4 Gun position at Batterie Moltke. (Author's collection)

Below: No. 4 Gun in May 1945 after liberation – the white sheet was placed across the barrel by the German forces stationed there to show they were surrendering. (Courtesy of the Channel Islands Occupation Society (Jersey))

Above: Two barrels lay in the naval gun emplacement at No. 4 Gun. (Author's collection)

Below: The internal rooms of the gun position are full of artefacts from the occupation. (Author's collection)

Above: As you exit No. 4 Gun position you can make out the boot imprints of the workers who laid the original concrete. (Author's collection)

Below: A view of the MP3 Naval Direction and Range-Finding Tower from the Coastal Artillery Range-Finding Position at Les Landes. (Author's collection)

4. Battle of the Flowers

The Battle of the Flowers is a spectacular two-day annual event that takes place on the second Thursday and Friday in August on Victoria Avenue in St Helier. The festival, one of the largest float carnivals in Europe, sees each parish of the island being responsible for creating a main float – which are adorned with flowers, thousands of them! These days, the event can attract around 20,000 spectators, with music, marching bands, dancers, funfairs, majorettes, street performers and plenty of food and drink to go with the parade of flower floats. It began well over 100 years ago in 1902, when a parade was organised to celebrate the coronation of King Edward VII and Queen Alexandra. Those original floats were mainly horse-drawn and the tradition at the time was for flowers and petals to be torn from the float and thrown to a lady in the crowd, in the hope that one would be thrown back! These days, the daytime afternoon parade has motorised floats that can be well over 35–40 feet in length, with prizes awarded in numerous different categories. Since 1989, there has also been a Moonlight Parade on the Friday, which begins after dark, with the floats lit up by literally thousands of lights, and ending with a fireworks display over St Aubin's Bay. The time and effort that goes into creating these floats must be substantial and the whole 'battle' is a real feast for the senses and well worth experiencing.

Just one of the many floats in Jersey's Battle of the Flowers. (Courtesy of Dave Sewell)

5. Beauport Beach

It's fair to say that Jersey has its fair share of glorious beaches and one of them is the hidden gem of Beauport beach. Located on the south-west of the island, just a mile from the more popular and well-known St Brelade's Bay, Beauport offers a much more isolated and relaxed beach environment. There is a small car park high up that soon gets full by those wishing to walk along the coastal path as well as those going to the beach. A steep set of steps and pathway is the only way down the cliff face from the car park, and as there are no facilities whatsoever at the destination, it is essential you take everything you're going to need! However, it's worth it, as this south facing secluded beach is arguably the most picturesque in the whole of Jersey! The unspoilt sand is surrounded on three sides by impressive granite cliffs that seemingly stretch up forever, providing shelter from any wind and creating the perfect sun trap. Add to this clear and calm turquoise waters, just right for swimming in, and you have yourself all you need for a relaxing day. Whether you are looking to simply soak up the sun or build sandcastles whilst searching for pirate treasure amongst the rocks, Beauport is worth a visit. The bay is a popular anchor spot for private and small tourist boats, so keep your eyes peeled as you never know which celebrity you may be sharing the sand with!

The walk down to the secluded Beauport beach. (Author's collection)

Pristine golden sands await you on Beauport beach. (Author's collection)

6. Bergerac

There can only be a handful of television shows and characters that are instantly synonymous with a location, and *Bergerac*, with its immediately recognisable theme tune, is one. Produced by the BBC and the Australian Seven Network, the show ran for nine series from 1981 to 1991 featuring the actor John Nettles in the lead role of Detective Jim Bergerac. The show utilised everything that Jersey had to offer, with location shots showcasing the beaches, climate and culture of the island to an audience of over 10 million each week – this was of course in the days before online streaming and satellite and cable channels. The programme acted as a large marketing tool for tourism to the island – and it is not surprising that visitor numbers increased over the years. The soundtrack to *Bergerac*, created by renowned composer George Fenton, instantly takes you to Jersey anytime you hear it, and the ten years that the programme was on for have certainly helped cement Jersey, and Bergerac, into a generation's memory. It is still possible to easily visit the vast majority of locations used in the series.

John Nettles, the star of *Bergerac*, in a Jersey tourism advert. (Courtesy of Jersey Tourism CC BY 2.0)

7. Bouley Bay Beach

Nestled in amongst the tallest cliffs on the island's north coast, Bouley Bay is a lovely small harbour that stretches around for about 2 miles. Although mostly made up of pebbles, there is a small sandy shelf that then plunges into deep blue waters that provide deep anchorage for boats. When the tide recedes, there are rock pools aplenty just waiting to be explored, and the green cliffs at either end are a haven for birds and other wildlife. The bay itself looks out towards the Normandy coast and the pier can be a good spot for fishing. In days gone by, it is known that Bouley Bay was a favourite spot for smugglers to bring their goods ashore and sitting in the Black

A view of Bouley Bay. (Courtesy of Andy Hawkins CC BY-SA 2.0)

Dog pub for some light refreshment, it is easy to imagine the comings-and-goings at this secluded harbour over the years. The area is also used for the Bouley Bay Hill Climb, a well-known motorsports event that is organised by the Jersey Motorcycle and Light Car Club, which takes place on the winding roads that surround the harbour and bring competitors from all over the world.

8. Channel Islands Military Museum

Located towards the northern end of St Ouen's Bay, the Channel Islands Military Museum is a fantastic museum that is actually housed in a former 10.5 cm casemate that was part of Hitler's Atlantic Wall defences on the island. Nestled just in behind the seawall, the main 10.5 cm gun overlooked the wide expanse of sand that stretched for 3 miles along Jersey's west coast. During the Nazi occupation of 1940–45, a twelve-man crew would have manned the position day and night, and the fact that the museum building itself is one of the exhibits only adds to the impressive nature of the collection. Inside, every inch is used to showcase German and civilian items from the occupation. From uniforms to guns, ordinance to official documentation, and plenty of personal items and recounts, this is a museum that tells the story of what life was like for the local population, and the German troops stationed here, under the five years of occupation. It is poignantly presented, with the personal details and photographs really bringing home the impact of those turbulent years.

A wartime picture of the bunker – it is just possible to make out camouflaged trees painted on the defensive wall. (Courtesy of Damien Horn, The Channel Islands Military Museum)

Above: A view of the bunker today – now The Channel Islands Military Museum. (Author's collection)

Below: Each room inside the bunker is jam-packed with artefacts from the occupation. (Author's collection)

9. Devil's Hole

Located in the north-west of the island in the parish of St Mary, Devil's Hole is a large natural blowhole that stretches approximately 100 feet across and over 200 feet down! Formed over thousands of years, the power of the sea gradually eroded the roof of a cave until it collapsed, leaving this rather strange and eerie-looking crater.

A view of Devil's Hole, sometime between 1890 and 1900.

Originally known as 'Le Creux de Vis' or Spiral Cave, it was only in the nineteenth century that the name of Devil's Hole was used, and this might be because of what happened in 1851, when the figurehead from the French shipwreck *La Joséphine* was washed into the hole and a local sculptor turned it into a wooden devil. Today, the cliff path winds its way down to a safe viewing platform and passes a 20-foot-high metal devil statue, said to be based on the wooden one, on the way. Whatever the weather, watching the waves crash through the tunnel entrance onto the rocks below can be a mesmerising experience.

10. Elizabeth Castle

Lying within St Aubin's Bay and a stone's throw away from the capital, St Helier, is a small island that is cut off from the mainland by the tide twice a day called L'Islet. Adjacent to this is a small outcrop of rocks where a Belgium monk named Helerius landed in around AD 550 and established a small hermitage. From here, he converted Jersey's population to Christianity, before later being killed by sea-going raiders, and from this point the hermitage became a prominent place of pilgrimage. Centuries later, in 1155, an Abbey of Saint Helier was founded on L'Islet, and remained operating until it was forcibly closed during the Reformation. With that, the Crown seized the monastic buildings, and they were then fortified to create a new defensive position.

The development of weaponry in the sixteenth century meant that the existing stronghold on the island at Mont Orgueil was no longer sufficient to defend Jersey. A newer, stronger bastion was needed, and with the vital port of St Helier now vulnerable from attack by ships armed with new cannons, the tidal island of L'Islet sat at the mouth of the harbour seemed the perfect place to build.

Work developing the site began in 1594, with the Upper Ward and the Queen Elizabeth Gate being completed first. Once complete, Sir Walter Raleigh, who was the Governor of Jersey between 1600 and 1603, named the castle Elizabeth Castle after Queen Elizabeth I of England, and moved the Governor's official place of residence from Mont Orgueil to the new castle. The building work was far from over however, and by 1636 the Lower Ward was constructed on what was the site of the former abbey church – with a portion of the former church now becoming a storeroom. A large barrack building, along with a separate officers' quarters, were built around a central parade ground, and wells and cisterns were dug into the rock for water.

When the English Civil War erupted in 1642, it wasn't long before the great stronghold of Elizabeth Castle became embroiled with it. In March 1643, Sir Philippe de Carteret, the Seigneur of St Ouen and also the island's Lieutenant Governor and Bailiff, retreated to the castle after a number of locals prevented him from reading out a letter from the king to the States and in the April of that year, the castle's guns opened fire on nearby Parliamentarian ships in the bay. Sir Philippe died in August 1643, and his son-in-law Sir George Carteret took over his roles. He managed to reduce and expel the Parliamentarian faction.

Between April and June 1646, Charles, the Prince of Wales, visited the castle and then returned three years later in September 1649 as King Charles II. He was the eldest surviving child of Charles I, who had been executed in January 1649. The Parliament of Scotland proclaimed Charles II king on 5 February 1649, and a few days later, on 17 February 1649, the Bailiff of Jersey, George Carteret, also proclaimed him king, as well as offering him asylum on the island. Knowing that Carteret had a small private army made up of Royalist veterans who had fled from England after the defeat of Charles I, along with a collection of foreign mercenaries, he accepted, and moved into Elizabeth Castle.

In October 1651, Parliamentarian forces inevitably landed in Jersey and bombarded the castle with mortars. Admiral Blake's fleet escorted over 2,500 troops to the island and lay siege to the island. Besieged for seven weeks, a shell crashed through the roof of the old medieval abbey church in the heart of the castle complex, which had been used as the storehouse for ammunition and provisions, and two years of supplies were gone. Carteret was forced to surrender on 15 December 1651 and Jersey was then held by the Parliamentarians for the next nine years until the restoration of the monarchy.

The strategic location of the castle saw more improvements added to it, which only enhanced its reputation as Jersey's foremost defensive position. During the Seven Years' War (1756–63), French prisoners were kept at the island, and a few years later during the Battle of Jersey in 1781, the castle garrison refused to surrender to the French, who were eventually defeated. However, this incident highlighted the potential weakness of a castle that is surrounded by sea for seven hours out of every twelve, as it meant that the troops at Elizabeth Castle were unable to effectively defend St Helier when cut-off by the tide. This vulnerability led to the construction of Fort Regent on Mont de la Ville, and this in time became the site of the main British garrison.

In the early nineteenth century a two-storey hospital was built, as well as a breakwater linking L'Islet to Hermitage Rock. At the turn of the twentieth century, the castle's usefulness as a military location diminished significantly, and the British government withdrew the garrison and sold the castle to the States of Jersey in 1923 for £1,500, who then opened the site to the public as a museum.

It did see a return to active service during the Second World War, when the Germans occupied the Channel Islands and used forced labourers to modernise the castle with various guns, bunkers and battlements. After the Liberation, the castle was repaired and eventually reopened to the public, run by Jersey Heritage.

Visiting Elizabeth Castle is an exhilarating experience, not just because of its size, but also because of the approach. At low tide, you can walk the causeway out to the main gate, whilst at all other times you will need to take an amphibious vehicle!

The castle is split into three sections: the Upper Ward; the Lower Ward and the Outer Ward.

Entering through the main gate, there is a guard house constructed in 1810, as well as the small and much older Fort Charles, which was built in 1647 during the English Civil War. Named after the Prince of Wales, who was on the island at the time, it was constructed to cover the approach to the castle from the causeway. Further up there is the Second Gate and West Bastion, as well as the Hospital Block, built in 1810. Just below this is a searchlight bunker, constructed by German forces during the Second World War, to house a powerful searchlight that could move along rails to the North-East Bastion near the entrance, and overlooking the approach to the docks at St Helier. The 1640 laid bowling green stretches up towards the impressive Grand Battery, which was armed with fifteen 24-pound cannons, and to the side of this is a more recent 10.5 cm casemate.

The Lower Ward was constructed by 1636 and utilised the original buildings from the priory church that had been there for hundreds of years. A large parade ground dominates this section of the castle, with a large soldiers' barracks capable of accommodating a staggering 480 men in 1798 on one side, and an officers' quarters for twelve on the other. There are plenty of stores and other buildings here, with a 1940 German 10.5 cm casemate built into the Royal Bastion, which has an impressive range card painted on its walls. From the Lower Ward you can walk out to the small harbour that connects to the Hermitage.

The Upper Ward was the most heavily defended part of the castle and is a maze of winding stairways and narrow alleys. Passing through the Iron Gate and Queen Elizabeth Gate, complete with her coat of arms, you arrive at the lower keep, which has been embellished by a German gun position. Further around is the Captain's House and Governor's House, before you twist your way up to the Upper Keep Bastion with its two traversing guns and Mount Battery, which was added to during the Second World War occupation with a Fire Control Tower.

A visit to Elizabeth Castle today allows you to see these different layers of history, and you get a very real sense of what it would have been like here all those years ago. It is easily possible to spend an entire day here, not just exploring the maze of rooms, walkways and battlements, but taking in the exhibits and stunning views offered at every vantage point.

Elizabeth Castle. (Courtesy of Tobias Scheck CC BY 2.0)

Above: A view of the Grand Battery, with the Lower and Upper Ward behind, from the Green. (Author's collection)

Below: A 6 pound gun, used by re-enactors as part of their display, sits in an area known as the cockpit. (Author's collection)

Above: Looking out towards the breakwater and the Hermitage. (Author's collection)

Below: A 1940 German 10.5 cm casemate built into the Royal Bastion still has its range card painted on the walls. (Author's collection)

The Second World War German Fire Control Tower on the top of Mount Battery. (Author's collection)

11. Faldouet Dolmen

There are a number of prehistoric dolmens and passage graves right across Jersey, and the 6,000-year-old La Pouquelaye d'Faldou is one of the best preserved and most complete. This Neolithic passage grave was first officially documented in the seventeenth century and has been excavated a number of times over the centuries; with human remains, pottery, axes and pendants all being uncovered. The 5-metre-long granite stone passageway leads to a double chamber. The first chamber is surrounded by a number of smaller side chambers, whilst the end chamber is still covered by a huge capstone – estimated to weigh a staggering 24 tons! Built sometime between 4000 and 3250 BC, it aligns with the rising sun on the spring and autumn equinox and was originally surrounded by some drystone walls, as well as a ring of upright stones – evidence of some of the walls can still easily be seen near the entrance. Located in an isolated place, surrounded by nothing but crops and mother nature, it is impossible not to feel something of the mysticism of this prehistoric site when the wind whips up and blows across the ancient stones.

La Pouquelaye d'Faldou. (Courtesy of Nicky Sewell)

12. Fort Leicester

Commanding the western end of Bouley Bay there has been some sort of defensive position here since 1549, when the French landed and occupied Sark, leading to the governor of the time, Sir Anthony Paulet, advising that a gun should be placed at 'La Radde du Boullay'. Bouley Bay was of strategic importance as it was a natural haven for vessels to anchor in, and by 1745 the single gun that was originally there had been added to and the site had been slowly developed into a battery. Named after the Queen's favourite, the Earl of Leicester, by 1795, it had a 12 pounder gun, along with a seaward and a landward wall and a guardhouse to the south of the site.

Fort Leicester was maintained and manned by the Jersey Militia, and by the 1830s it was significantly improved in order to accommodate five new heavy 32 pounder cannons. With a range of around 2 miles, these would have been positioned to prevent an enemy landing on the western side of Bouley Bay, and the newly constructed L'Etacquerel Fort protecting the eastern side of the bay. A company of around thirty men would have likely been needed to operate all these weapons. During the Second World War, occupying German forces added a searchlight and more modern gun emplacements in order to protect Bouley Bay. Since then, Fort Leicester has had a number of owners, but significantly, in 2005, ownership was transferred to the Public of the Island of Jersey, and Jersey Heritage now operate the site as a heritage holiday let.

A view of Fort Leicester. (Courtesy of Bob Embleton CC BY-SA 2.0)

Looking down at Fort Leicester and the western side of Bouley Bay.

13. Grève de Lecq

Straddled between the parishes of St Mary and St Ouen, Grève de Lecq is one of the few sheltered bays along the North Coast of the island. Here, it seems that the tide never goes too far out from the beautiful yellow sands, and with some beachside cafés and pubs on hand for some refreshments, it can be a popular destination for many. However, this sheltered location has meant that there is more to Grève de Lecq than just the golden sands. In 1779, half of a French Expeditionary Force attempted to land here, forcing the governor at the time to order the rapid building of a guard house, battery and tower within a year, followed by an additional guardhouse and battery on the cliff at Le Câtel by 1789. Le Câtel Fort and Battery were soon joined by Middle Battery, Valle du Fort Battery and a round tower to protect the bay, and as a result Grève de Lecq Barracks was built in 1810 in order to accommodate the 250 men needed to man the positions – quite some building in a mere thirty years. It had two blocks for soldiers, each consisting of four barrack rooms – which would have meant twenty to twenty-five in a room, and two small rooms for non-commissioned officers, who had considerably more space and privacy. The last troops here were withdrawn in 1926 and over the next fifty years or so the site was simply left disused.

Above: Looking back towards Grève de Lecq beach.

Below: Grève de Lecq Barracks. (Courtesy of Bob Embleton CC BY-SA 2.0)

Today it is managed by the National Trust, and it is the only surviving barracks left on the north coast of the Island and retains many original features. As well as the barrack accommodation, which is now a number of holiday lets, surrounding the site are a number of associate buildings, including a coal store, two prison cells and the ablutions block – for those soldiers who had had a bit too much to drink!

14. Grosnez Castle

As far as spectacular locations go, Grosnez Castle is certainly up there – especially at sunset – but there's sadly very little left of Grosnez Castle now, aside from a few walls and an archway, but they do give us a tantalising glimpse of what the castle may have looked like when originally built. Protected on three sides by steep cliffs and crashing waves, the fourth landward side had thick high walls, two strong towers and a gatehouse, which allowed access across a dry moat. Likely to have been constructed around the early to mid-fourteenth century on the orders of Sir John des Roches, it was taken by invading French forces in 1373 and again in 1381. At first sight, the castle is seemingly in a very strong defensive position, but it actually had a number of weaknesses – there were few internal buildings for a garrison to stay in

Little now remains of Grosnez Castle. (Author's collection)

and no fresh water supply being two! In fact, these issues are likely to have led to its quick downfall, and it is thought that it was demolished sometime between 1460 and 1485, having stood for little over one hundred years.

15. Grouville Bay

Situated on the east coast of Jersey, Grouville Bay has a stunning wide, sandy beach that offers shallow, sheltered waters to swim in without the worry of strong currents. At its northern end is the small village of Gorey and its harbour, which of course has the spectacular Mont Orgueil Castle nestled in behind. There is a row of houses at the foot of the castle overlooking the harbour, and one of them was requisitioned by the Wehrmacht during the German occupation of the Second World War and converted into a disguised pillbox! To the south of Grouville is the Royal Jersey Golf

The sweeping sands of Grouville Bay come all the way around to Gorey harbour – as seen here from the top of Mont Orgueil. (Author's collection)

Club. Queen Victoria was so impressed with the area when she visited, it became known as the Royal Bay of Grouville, and it is easy to see why, with picture-perfect vistas in every direction you look!

16. Hamptonne Country Life Museum

Located in the parish of St Lawrence, Hamptonne Country Life Museum is a complex of different houses that offer the chance to discover Jersey's history of cider making, as well as having a glimpse of what rural life was like here over the centuries. Purchased in 1987 by the National Trust of Jersey, with the assistance of the States of Jersey, it was restored and refurbished by the Societe Jersiaise, before being operated by Jersey Heritage. The site comprises three houses, with each one dating from a different century, and they reflect how things have changed in Jersey over time. These houses are named after the families who have lived at Hamptonne, with the Syvret Building, Hamptonne House and the Langlois Building, along with an orchard and other outbuildings completing the site. Records show that a building

Hamptonne Country Life Museum.

was here as long ago as 1445 and walking around the site today, it feels very much like a traditional farm. Chickens, sheep, pigs, cows and local crafts are on display as are the various architectural features within the buildings. Of special mention is the annual cider making festival in October, called La Faîs'sie d'Cidre, which offers a good insight into Jersey cider making – and the opportunity to purchase some too!

17. Jersey Museum, Art Gallery and Victorian House

If you're looking for a little treasure trove of all things Jersey, then this museum in St Helier is a must. A large range of exhibits cover everything about the island, starting around 250,000 years ago when the first people arrived in Jersey, to the island's rich nature and its complex culture and history. The museum sheds light on the long links to the English Crown – despite being geographically so close to France. The island's traditional farming industry, archive footage of the early years of Jersey tourism and the German occupation during the Second World War are all covered – along

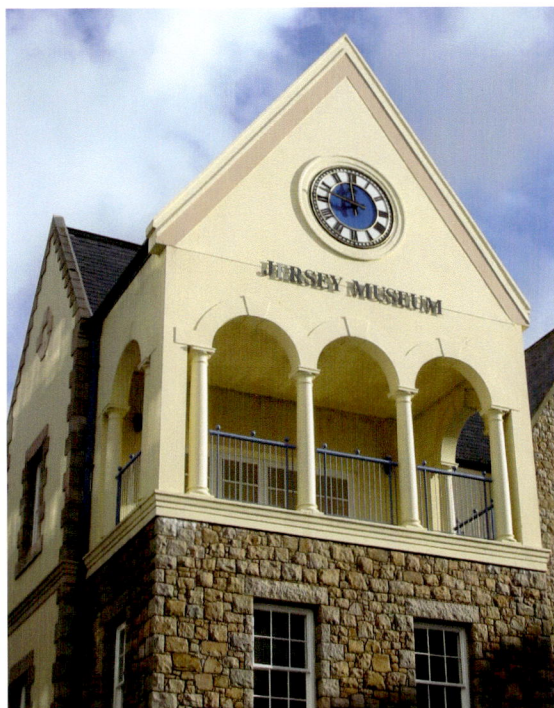

The external view of Jersey Museum, Art Gallery & Victorian House.

with examples of *Jèrriais* (the Jersey language) being spoken. Some impressive archaeological displays from the Neolithic period and an interesting permanent display; 'Jersey – 100 Objects' are well worth exploring. Linked to the museum is the beautifully restored Victorian House. Stepping inside the gaslit home is incredibly atmospheric, and the personal story of a Victorian family in crisis as *Dr Charles Ginestet* abandons their beautiful home and flees to France to start a new life adds a human element to it all. On the ground floor is an exhibition entitled 'Trade Roots', which looks at the evidence of the island's involvement in the transatlantic slave trade. A fascinating museum and house which certainly go a long way to explaining Jersey's history and heritage.

18. Jersey War Tunnels

When German forces occupied the island during the Second World War, they decided to construct a vast network of tunnels using forced and slave workers from nations across Europe. The network would allow the safe storage of munitions and food, as well as allowing the troops to withstand potential Allied air raids and bombardment. Known as Hohlgangsanlage 8 (abbreviated to Ho8), some of the nearly 1 km of

The entrance to the Jersey War Tunnels. (Courtesy of Matt Kieffer CC BY-SA 2.0)

tunnels that go up to 50 metres underground were then converted into a casualty clearing station and emergency hospital in late 1943 to early 1944 as it became clear there was likely to be an Allied invasion of Europe. At this point unfinished tunnels were sealed off and an air conditioning and heating system was installed for the 500-bed hospital – complete with operating theatre. However, it was never used as intended. The Allies bypassed the Channel Islands when liberating Europe in June 1944 and after the war Ho8 fell into disrepair. The tunnels ultimately fell under private ownership based on who owned the land above which they were built, and this saw the complex gradually being restored, with a museum and memorial to the occupation being set up originally as the German Underground Hospital. Now known as the Jersey War Tunnels, you can visit and experience what life would have been like working in the underground hospital, as well as explore the number of different exhibits, focusing on daily life for those on Jersey, cooperation and resistance with the enemy and liberation. There are numerous artefacts and visual displays throughout, but it is the echoey footsteps as you meander the tunnels that really bring home what it would have been like here during the occupation.

19. Jersey Wetland Centre

The Jersey Wetland Centre officially opened in 2014, although the site has been looked after by the National Trust for Jersey since 1975 and gives anyone the opportunity to view some of the diverse bird life found here. Located on the west of the island, it overlooks La Mare au Seigneur, better known as St Ouen's Pond, which is the largest area of natural open water in Jersey. The name of La Mare au Seigneur is thought to date back to 1309 when the local seigneur kept its carps in the pond and used the surrounding land as a hunting ground! Excitingly, the centre is accessed by

The entrance to the Jersey Wetland Centre. (Author's collection)

a tunnel – which goes through a large sand dune mound, before coming out on the other side with the perfect view of reeds and the pond. From here in the observation room and its viewing windows, birdwatchers can observe the wetland habitats and watch the marsh harriers, waders and waterfowl without disturbing them. This is an SSI (site of special interest) nature reserve that is not only a modern bird-hide, but also acts as an interpretation centre, allowing the whole family to learn about the reserve and its wildlife thanks to the exhibits describing the local wildlife, flora and fauna.

20. Jersey Zoo

Jersey Zoo was opened in March 1959 as Durrell Wildlife Park, and it has been welcoming thousands of visitors every year since. It was the idea of author and conservationist Gerald Durrell (1925–95) who wanted a more 'diverse, beautiful and resilient natural landscapes in which species can thrive and people can enjoy a deeper connection with nature'. Since 1964, the zoo has been home to the Durrell Wildlife Conservation Trust (formerly the Jersey Wildlife Preservation Trust) and this is who continues to operate the zoo today. Located at Les Augrès Manor, in the parish of Trinity, it covers 32 acres and has over 130 different species of mammals, birds, amphibians and reptiles. As well as housing a number of rare and endangered species, the zoo has some large areas within the grounds for native habitat areas. Like most zoos and wildlife parks, there are different sections for the different creatures.

Some of the buildings at Jersey Zoo. (Courtesy of Jersey Tourism CC BY 2.0)

The Gaherty Reptile and Amphibian Centre, named after Canadian philanthropist Geoff Gaherty, houses a number of reptiles and amphibians including iguanas, tortoise, pythons and a number of frogs – including the Amazon poison dart frog! The Cloud Forest has sloth, bears and howler monkey whilst the Jewels of the Forest is home to a whole range of Asian birds, including the Java sparrow and the white-rumped shama. The Discovery Desert has aardvarks and meerkats, and the Central Valley provides a home to a number of local species such as kingfishers and dragonflies. Walking around the rest of the site you can find lemurs, tamarins, marmosets, gorillas, orangutans and gibbons, as well as numerous aviaries!

But Jersey Zoo is more than just a nature reserve. There is a real commitment and drive here to educate others and provide specialist support. The Princess Royal Pavilion acts as a conference centre and classroom and Jersey Zoo is a leader in 'animal husbandry, research, training and education' – and it is through this that they are able to deliver endangered species breeding. Jersey Zoo are also able to provide 'specialist training to enable conservationists and partner organisations to become more effective'.

21. La Corbière Lighthouse

Instantly recognisable as one of Jersey's most iconic landmarks, La Corbière Lighthouse is a must-see destination for anyone visiting the island. The numerous rocks and large tidal differences around this part of Jersey's coast has seen many shipwrecks and loss of life over the years – which led to the need to install a lighthouse. Situated at the most south-westerly point of Jersey in the parish of St Brelade, a causeway links the shore of Jersey to the lighthouse. Designed by Sir John Coode, La Corbière was completed in 1874 as the first concrete-built lighthouse in Britain. Standing 19 metres high, the lamp is 36 metres above the high-water mark and its beam can reach 18 nautical miles (33 km). Although fully automated in 1976, a plaque next to the causeway commemorates Peter Edwin Larbalestier, the assistant keeper of the lighthouse, who sadly drowned on 28 May 1946 while trying to rescue a visitor to the causeway who had got cut off by the incoming tide. Today there is an alarm to warn visitors to clear the causeway as the tide starts to rise. On the headland overlooking the lighthouse, a monument commemorates the 1997 rescue of all 307 passengers from the French catamaran *Saint-Malo*, which ran aground 900 metres from the lighthouse. La Corbière lighthouse has to be one of the most photographed landmarks in Jersey, thanks to its panoramic views.

Opposite: The lighthouse is perched on a tidal rock and stands 19 metres high. (Author's collection)

Below: The causeway to La Corbière Lighthouse when the tide is out. (Author's collection)

La Corbière Lighthouse became fully automated in 1976. (Author's collection)

22. La Crête Fort

Built on a headland between Bonne Nuit Bay and Giffard Bay, La Crête Fort is a small defensive fort dating from the late eighteenth/early nineteenth century. The review of Jersey's defences in 1778 recommended the creation of a battery at La Crête, and a small two-gun battery was constructed. The small battery has a guardhouse to its rear and would have originally had a ditch surrounding it. In 1834 the fort was improved with a new magazine that would have likely housed two 18 pounder guns and four 12 pounders, as well as a better guardhouse, providing a good base for the thirty or so men that would be stationed here. In 1848 it received an upgrade and housed six 32 pounder cannons – and this is the structure of the fort that remains today. By the end of the nineteenth century it was abandoned, but during the German Occupation of the Second World War, the fort was reinforced and manned by a small contingent of troops. A 3.7 cm PAK anti-tank gun, mortar, several machine guns and a searchlight were installed, although these were never used in anger. Today, La Crête Fort is managed by Jersey Heritage and run as a holiday let.

23. La Hougue Bie Museum

You cannot fail to be impressed by what is said to be one of the ten oldest buildings in the entire world! Estimated to have been built at some point between 4000 and 3500 BC, La Hougue Bie is one of largest and best-preserved passage graves in Europe. As you amble around the mound you suddenly appreciate its height of just over 12 metres when you come to the opening to the passage grave. Ducking down and arching your back as you enter, you cannot help but to walk in silence down the 18-metre tunnel towards the centre of the mound. As your footsteps echo and the temperature drops, you can imagine Neolithic people coming here for rituals, and excavations in 1925 found shards of vases and a scattering of human remains. The passage is aligned with sunrise at both the spring and summer equinox, and it is impossible not to marvel at the building techniques of our ancient ancestors. In the twelfth and sixteenth centuries, two separate small chapels were constructed on top of the mound, and a walk up to the top offers some stunning views across open countryside. The rest of the site is worth walking around and exploring as there is a fantastic reconstruction of a Neolithic house that allows you to get a snapshot of life thousands of years ago. An informative museum houses more information, including Le Câtillon II, the world's largest Celtic hoard of a staggering 70,000 coins and items of jewellery.

Despite the thousands of years of history, La Hougue Bie's prominent high position meant it did not escape the attention of German occupying forces during the Second

World War. In 1942, they constructed a steel observation tower on the top of the ancient mound and attached to the medieval chapel, whilst also building a bunker underground and installing machine-gun positions, trenches and barbed wire in the surrounding area. The observation post was taken down after the war, although the bases for the legs are still visible by the side of the chapel, but the underground bunker remained, and was turned into a permanent memorial dedicated to the forced workers brought to the island to construct the various German defences during the conflict. Walking down into the bunker is a sombre and quiet experience. Underground there are details of the twelve worker camps that were in Jersey, along with individual stories of camp inmates, and locals who tried to help them – some of them, like Mrs Louisa Gould, who were found to be sheltering escaped workers paid for their heroism with their life.

The Neolithic site of La Hougue Bie. (Author's collection)

Above: The entrance to the nearly 19-metre-long passage chamber. (Author's collection)

Below: A view of the two medieval chapels on top of the mound. (Author's collection)

This bunker is now a memorial dedicated to the suffering and courage of those transported to the Channel Islands...

The German Second World War bunker at La Hougue Bie stands as a memorial to workers from across Europe who were forced to build defences in Jersey during the German occupation. (Author's collection)

24. La Rocco Tower

La Rocco Tower was one of a number of coastal defensive towers built on Jersey to protect the island from a potential French attack, with a large number still standing. Originally called 'Gordon's Tower' after the Lieutenant-General Andrew Gordon, it was constructed between 1796 and 1801 and its role was to guard the vast expanse of sand at St Ouen's Bay from its small offshore tidal island. La Rocco was the twenty-third and last coastal tower in Jersey to be

A view of La Rocco Tower from the beach. (Author's collection)

A close-up of La Rocco Tower. (Courtesy of Bob Embleton CC BY-SA 2.0)

built – it was also the largest and most heavily armed. In 1848, it was recorded as having five 32 pounder guns, but by the end of the nineteenth century it had been decided that it was no longer a useful military site. In 1896 it was included in a list of War Department properties identified as available for disposal, and the States of Jersey purchased the site in 1923 for £100, for the purpose of providing a landmark for passing shipping due to the precarious rocks that lie along the west coast of the island. During the Second World War, German forces identified St Ouen's Bay as the most likely point of a potential Allied invasion of Jersey, and they put landmines around the tower, which were wired to La Braye slipway. In 1943 the accidental detonation of some of these landmines inflicted much damage to the tower, and this wasn't fully rectified until 1972. It is completely cut off by the tide twice a day and is under the stewardship of Jersey Heritage, who offer the tower as a rather unique self-catering experience! However, for most visitors, La Rocco Tower provides an iconic silhouette over the beautiful St Ouen's Bay.

25. La Rocque Harbour

La Rocque Harbour is another one of those delightful little locations on Jersey that offer a whole range of differing views over the course of a day. A breakwater offers protection to this working fishing harbour and its boats, and at high tide there is no sand visible. But as the water recedes, miles and miles of beach are gradually exposed, along with numerous rock pools that are perfect for exploring. Good local facilities mean that it is easily possible to spend a whole day here with the family.

La Rocque Harbour at high tide.

26. Le Dolmen du Couperon

For an island of only 45 square miles, Jersey certainly has a large number of Neolithic sites, and Le Dolmen du Couperon is one of them. Believed to be around 4,500 years old, it is thought that the 8-metre-long dolmen was once covered by a mound of earth. Between 1868 and 1919 excavations were carried out and archaeologists recovered and repositioned fallen stones to the way they stand today. Located right by the side of the dolmen is a guardhouse that was built and maintained for centuries by the local Jersey Militia to help protect this part of the island. Its isolated location in a field overlooking cliffs and to the east of Rozel Bay adds to the spiritual feeling of this site.

Le Dolmen du Couperon and guardhouse. (Courtesy of A Ronin CC BY-SA 3.0)

27. L'Etacquerel Fort

L'Etacquerel Fort was built on a headland overlooking Bouley Bay in 1836. Although an earlier battery had been built nearby between 1786 and 1790, it was modified by adding a guardhouse and flanking screen walls to add additional protection. Actually built into the rock itself, the seaward wall sits roughly 50 metres above high-tide, whilst on the landward side, an impressive 21-foot-deep dry defensive ditch was dug. A small wooden bridge crosses the ditch to an entrance area that contains a guardhouse for a small number of men. There were three traversing gun platforms, and the whole plan was for these guns to work in tandem with the guns at Fort Leicester to the west to protect Bouley Bay. Over the years, the fort became disused, largely in part to its isolated position that made it difficult to access. Today it is maintained by Jersey Heritage, who offer a unique self-catering experience for those wishing to get away from modern living for a bit. There is no running water or electricity on site, but being surrounded on three sides by plunging cliffs offer this location peace and quiet – and impressive views!

L'Etacquerel Fort overlooking Bouley Bay.

28. Le Hocq Tower

When the threat of a French invasion seemed imminent in the mid- to late eighteenth century, a series of defensive round towers were constructed on the orders of the Governor of Jersey, General Henry Seymour Conway, and Le Hocq is one of these. Likely completed in 1781, the 11-metre diameter structure was divided up into three levels: the ground floor for storage (including the gunpowder) and the other two floors acting as the living quarters for the ten men who were stationed here. There would have been an 18 pounder carronade on a wooden traversing platform mounted on the roof, with another two or three 18 pounder cannons next to the tower on a small paved area. Although it fell into disuse by the beginning of the twentieth century, the Germans occupying the island during the Second World War did replace the wooden floors with concrete ones in order to strengthen the tower, and they manned it for the duration of the conflict. Today, Le Hocq Tower has a rather distinctive white patch painted on its seaward side to act as a daymark for shipping navigation.

Le Hocq Tower. (Courtesy of Ruben Holthuijsen CC BY 2.0)

29. Le Petit Train

If you're looking for a leisurely way to explore the whole of St Aubin's Bay, then Le Petit Train is something you have to do! Running seven days a week from April to October, two land trains accommodating up to sixty people link Liberation Square in St Helier to the parish hall at St Aubin, with an additional stop en route at West Park. Taking approximately thirty-five minutes from end to end, the train follows the promenade cycle path that is adjacent to the sea wall and provides a commentary on all the sights you can see along the way, detailing their history and importance. Even inclement weather won't stop your enjoyment, as transparent sides can be rolled down allowing you to stay dry and enjoy the ride as you pass Elizabeth Castle, the Glass Church, as well as numerous bunkers and anti-tank walls from the German occupation. Le Petit Train provides a wonderfully unique way of exploring this beautiful part of Jersey.

Right: What better way to travel around St Aubin's Bay than on Le Petit Train? (Courtesy of Nicola de Louche)

Below: Le Petit Train makes three stops on its way from St Aubin's to St Helier. (Courtesy of Nicola de Louche)

30. Liberation Square

Liberation Square was opened by the Prince of Wales as part of the fiftieth anniversary of the island's liberation from German occupation during the Second World War. The *Monument to Freedom* statue is a rather poignant sculpture of locals waving a large Union Flag at the moment of the Liberation of Jersey on 9 May 1945. The location chosen is significant. The main building here had been taken over by occupying forces and made into the German Harbour Office, and it was from the first-floor window of that building that the first Allied troops who landed on the island on 9 May 1945 lowered a Union Flag – signifying the end of five years of German occupation.

Liberation Square. (Author's collection)

31. Maritime Museum

The Maritime Museum has to be one of the best museums for families that I have had the pleasure to discover, and come rain or shine, this is a gem well worth exploring. Set in some old warehouses in the harbour area of St Helier, the Maritime Museum was opened in 1997 and covers the islands' rich history of shipbuilding and life surrounded by the sea. Inside, it is like a treasure trove of artefacts, from the figureheads of ships, information about knots, cannons, and model ships to look at, but there is so much more. This is very much a hands-on museum, and it is the sheer number of different and interesting interactive displays that will occupy the children for hours. From finding out about the impact of high and low tide on the island to building your own boat; and from using a wind cannon to demonstrate how sails work to getting wet with small boats on a mini ocean, there is fun and learning at every turn. A genuine piece of the island's Second World War history is also on display, with the small boat *Diana* on show – a local boat that helped rescue stranded troops from St Malo as German forces advanced on the port.

Also within the museum site is the impressive *Occupation Tapestry*, which was unveiled at the fiftieth anniversary of the island's liberation from German occupying forces in 1995. There are twelve separate panels, representing the twelve parishes of the island, each measuring 6 feet by 3 feet and showing various aspects of life during the Second World War. Later on, a thirteenth panel was added to mark the seventieth

The Maritime Museum has a vast amount of fabulous hands-on activities to keep the whole family entertained. (Author's collection)

On display in the Maritime Museum is the boat *Diana*, which helped rescue troops from St Malo as German forces advanced on the port in the Second World War. (Author's collection)

Just one of the stunning panels of the Occupation Tapestry. (Author's collection)

anniversary of the liberation. The tapestry is on display in a separate gallery that has no natural light in order to protect and preserve it. This certainly adds to the poignancy of it, with the dimly lit room providing a solemn chamber in which to look at the incredible craftsmanship of the tapestry, read the information panels and contemplate what life was like for the islanders during the occupation.

32. Mont Orgueil Castle

If you are looking for an iconic castle that dominates its surroundings and is steeped in history, then this is it! Sat overlooking Gorey harbour on the east of Jersey, Mont Orgueil was originally constructed between 1204 and 1212 as the islands chose to remain loyal to the Norman duke, John (who was also the King of England), as a power struggle with the French king, Philip II Augustus, loomed on the horizon. Built on a rocky ridge, which was the site of an old Iron Age hill fort, it was a large undertaking, and the ramparts and towers were soon strengthened in 1224.

Over the next 400 years the castle was subjected to a number of attacks by French forces, and being the main fortress in Jersey, it went through a number of improvements and developments. In July 1373, the Constable of France, Bertrand du Guesclin, attacked the castle with an estimated force of 2,000 men. By concentrating his firepower on one part of the castle, he managed to breach the Outer Ward walls. However, the garrison retreated to the inner parts of the castle, which the French could not breach, and the fighting continued until a relief force from England arrived. Although the castle itself was strong, and protected Gorey harbour well, other parts of the island were less secure, and the French continued to raid the island.

Also known as Gorey Castle, it was 'taken' by the French in 1461, although it was more of a transfer of power as Margaret of Anjou, the French-born wife of Henry VI of England, seemingly handed control of the island over in return for French aid and assistance during the Wars of the Roses. This didn't last long, however, as the castle was retaken in 1468 by an English relief force.

The development of cannon warfare led to much needed renovation taking place, as the castle would now be susceptible from a landward attack – particularly from the hill to the west. Platforms for artillery were built in the mid-sixteenth century; the keep was extended into a D-shaped bastion in 1551, which was better against artillery fire; and a large L-shaped Grand Battery, facing west, was constructed in 1560. However, despite these vast improvements, by 1600 Elizabeth Castle was now the primary defensive position on Jersey and Walter Raleigh moved the governor's official place of residence from Mont Orgueil to the new castle overlooking St Helier.

The castle was used as a prison in the 1600s and during the English Civil War, it was from Mont Orgueil that the Royalists, under Sir George Carteret, retook the island from the Parliamentarian forces in November 1643. By the end of the seventeenth century the castle was in a ruinous state, and it wasn't until 1730–34 that some repairs were carried out. In the 1790s, the castle became the base for a French anti-revolutionary spy network named La Correspondance, and aside from housing a few troops over the years, this was the end of the castle's military life. It was formally handed to the people of Jersey in 1907 as an historic monument.

That was until the German occupation in the Second World War. They recognised the potential strategic location of Mont Orgueil, using rooms in the keep as a barracks and adding observation towers, trenches and gun positions, although they were never used in anger.

The castle itself is split into four sections: the Outer Ward, Lower Ward, Middle Ward and the keep.

The Outer Ward was a very large, enclosed area that was dominated by the curtain walls of the castle overlooking it. It was through this Outer Ward that anyone wishing to enter the castle would need to go through, and that is still the case today. The First Gate, which has the remains of the original thirteenth-century gate a few metres behind it, has the 1470 built Harliston Tower beside it.

Passing through the Outer Ward you finally reach the Second Gate, the entrance point to the Lower Ward. Built as a tower, before being turned into a gate, the room above it was used as a prison in the seventeenth and eighteenth centuries. The Lower Ward contained a number of associated buildings for the running of the castle, before many of them were cleared around 1800 to make room for a large parade ground. With Helie's Tower and the Southern Tower overlooking the harbour and the Cornish Bastion built into the curtain wall in 1547, this was a well defended area. Standing there today can feel the imposing walls of this ancient fortress looking down on you.

Above: Mont Orgueil sits above Gorey harbour. (Author's collection)

Below: A view of the Tudor Residential Apartments from the De Carteret Garden. (Author's collection)

A cannon in the Cornish Bastion overlooks the Second Gate, with Gorey harbour beyond. (Author's collection)

A German Second World War observation point at the top of Mont Orgueil. (Author's collection)

Left: There are numerous walkways and passages to explore. (Author's collection)

Below: The octagonal turret on Mount Battery was used as an observation post during the German occupation. (Author's collection)

The route to the keep winds its way through Queen Elizabeth Gate and into the Middle Ward, which has seen much redesign and redevelopment over the years. The Grand Battery was built here and there are the remains of the old chapel and a long cellar for storage. All of this within the shadow of the keep, and the more recent residential apartments. The Mount Gate offered those in the keep a final chance to keep invaders out – that is if they ever got that far, and beyond lay the medieval Great Hall, the undercroft and a number of towers that can see for miles around. The view from the top of the keep is spectacular. You are surrounded by huge walls and towers, with battlements and gun emplacements offering protection to those within. This is a vantage point that not only overlooks Gorey harbour but can also keep an eye on the stretch of water between Jersey and France.

33. Noirmont Point

In January 1947, Warren Farm and the Noirmont headland was purchased by the States of Jersey from Mrs Hope May Dixon, widow of William George Moore Dixon (Dame du Fief et Seigneurie de Noirmont) with the stipulation that 'it shall be preserved in perpetuity as a memorial to the men and women of Jersey who perished in

The older defensive tower, Tour de Vinde, at the foot of Noirmont Point. (Author's collection)

MP1 Naval Direction and Range-Finding Tower at Noirmont Point. (Author's Collection)

the Second World War'. The various bunkers associated with the German built Batterie Lothringen at Noirmont Point were sealed up in 1948 and lay abandoned for over thirty years, until the Channel Islands Occupation Society (CIOS) obtained permission to restore the command bunker and observation tower because of the historical significance of the site. A commemorative stone was installed on 9 May 1970 to mark the twentieth anniversary of the liberation of the island. At the foot of Noirmont Point is an older defensive tower called Tour de Vinde, which was built between 1810 and 1814 when the threat of a French invasion was at its peak, and just overlooking this is the impressive MP1 Naval Direction and Range-Finding Tower, built by German occupying forces in the Second World War. Standing at over 15 metres tall, it was built down into the cliff and is unique on the island as its entrance is on the top floor!

34. Pallot Steam Museum

Opened in 1990, the Pallot Steam Museum was established by a trust to showcase and preserve the incredible collection that Don Pallot (1910–96) had built up over

his lifetime. Interested in mechanics for his entire life, Don began collecting any number of machines, often having to restore them himself, and the collection serves as an incredible reference point of the island's heritage. From motorbikes to cars and from agricultural vehicles to steam rollers, the museum has a number of interesting, and often rare, items to view. Around the outskirts of the museum there is a standard gauge railway that it is possible to take a ride on. Departing from the Victorian style platform, it is like taking a real step back in time to the days of steam power.

35. Plemont Bay

On the north-west of Jersey lies the beautiful and unspoilt Plemont Bay. It is yet another stunning beach on the island but whether there is actually a beach to see does depend on when you visit! Plemont Bay is accessed down a rather steep stairway that passes the perfectly placed Plemont Beach Café. High tide is the ideal time to drop into the café, as the water completely covers the beach, leaving just large rocks to sit on if you so wish. However, low tide brings with it the unveiling of pristine golden sands that make the effort of all the steps very much worth it. The rather dramatic cliffs provide the beach a great deal of protection from any wind, and as the water goes further out exposing more sweeping sand, a great number of rock pools are left

Above: The secluded Plemont Bay. (Author's collection)

Below: The freshwater waterfall at Plemont Bay. (Author's collection)

just begging to be explored. If you've not been to the beach before, you are in for a treat, because as you clamber across the rocks and dip your toes into the pools, you suddenly become aware of a number of sea caves to explore. Eroded into the cliffs, it is impossible not to head into them, and with your voices echoing amongst the rocks, you feel like you are the first person to venture inside – with pirate treasure possibly lurking around every corner! The combination of the rocks, sand and seaweed can make it tricky under foot in places, but it is worth continuing to explore all around, as right at the very back by the towering cliff face is a stunning waterfall. It has cut back a small gully from the edge of the rocks over the centuries and the water pours over the edge dropping down into the chamber below. It is an inspiring thing to see, and it is almost impossible not to be mesmerised by it. For the more curious, you can go through the waterfall and peer out from behind. Add to this the shallow sea water at low tide and it is easy to understand why this is a popular destination for both tourists and locals. Just make sure you check those all-important tide times.

36. Portelet Bay

Portelet Bay is another seemingly perfect beach that is accessed by a number of steps over the side of a steep cliff. When parking at the public car park at the top, it is impossible to descend straight to the beach, without first taking in the incredible views that stretch on in all directions, and taking a number of photographs of the

A view of Portelet Bay. (Courtesy of Henry Burrows CC BY-SA 2.0)

sights you can see! The familiar golden sands of Jersey stretch all the way around the bay, with cliffs lush with green vegetation making this a lovely, sheltered sun trap. With a pub at the top and a beach café by the sand, refreshment is never too far away and as the tide goes out, numerous rock pools are revealed that are too good not to explore! The size of the beach and the fact that it is a little bit tricky to get to means that it is possible to find your own bit of sand a long way from anyone else. As well as the sand, the most striking feature of Portelet Bay is the Martello tower that stands on a small tidal island known as L'ile au Guerdain. This is Portelet Tower, built in the early nineteenth century to help project Jersey from French attack, and it is easy to see why this one was built where it was. Sitting right in the middle of the bay, it would have had a cannon and a garrison of over ten men to man it and stop an invading force from landing here. Predating the tower is the story of Phillipe Janvrin, a sea captain who died of the plague and whose body was buried here, which led to locals calling this La Tour Janvrin (Janvrin's Tower) or Janvrin's Tomb. The water recedes beyond Portelet Tower at low tide, and it is possible to walk across the sand and explore the single roomed tower at your leisure. Swimming, snorkelling and even fishing are all possible here, making Portelet Bay a gem well worth visiting.

37. Queen's Valley Reservoir

Although man-made, Queen's Valley Reservoir is now a haven for a variety of wildlife. Constructed in 1991, it holds gallons and gallons of untreated rainwater,

Queen's Valley Reservoir.

and is used to ensure the people of Jersey have a year-round supply of water. The vast majority of visitors here enjoy taking a quiet walk, or run, around the outskirts of the reservoir – which is just under 2 miles in length. Whilst doing so, there is plenty of natural splendour to keep you entertained – with a whole variety of birds, wildlife and vegetation at every corner. It is a very quiet place, and the perfect place to come and escape from the hustle and bustle of everyday life, with just the sound of the lapping water, rustling leaves and birdsong breaking the silence.

38. Resistance Nest, Millbrook

Located on Victoria Avenue, opposite the Old Station Café at Millbrook, this resistance nest is an excellent example of a 4.7 cm anti-tank gun casemate. It was deliberately built into the sea wall that overlooks St Aubin's Bay by the German occupying forces of the Second World War in an effort to camouflage it. The vast expanse of sand around St Aubin's Bay made it a potential landing zone for any Allied liberation attempt of Jersey and this resistance nest was just one of the defensive features built along this stretch of sea wall. A small group of around ten would have occupied this site with the aim of stopping any Allies that landed on the vast stretch of sand from getting off the beach. Armed with a light machine gun and one 4.7 cm Czechoslovakian anti-tank gun, this resistance nest is similar to many built right across the island. However, what sets it apart from the others is

Left: The Resistance Nest during the occupation, with barbed wire along the sea wall. (Courtesy of the Channel Islands Occupation Society (Jersey))

Below: A view of Millbrook today. (Author's collection)

The 4.7-cm Czech anti-tank gun inside the bunker. (Courtesy of the Channel Islands Occupation Society (Jersey))

the fact that immediately after the war it was sealed up and that is how it stayed until it was reopened in 1985. The Channel Islands Occupation Society (CIOS) have restored parts of it sympathetically – in a way that really allows a number of original features to really stand out. Because it was locked up soon after the war, much of the ventilation equipment is original, along with the electric cables, interior panelling and even some posters put up by the troops stationed here in the 1940s! Opened on specific days throughout the year, the small but immaculately preserved bunker is well worth a visit for anyone wishing to take a small step back in time.

39. Samares Manor and Botanical Gardens

There has been a dwelling of some sort at Samares in the south-east of the island since the twelfth century, but the manor house that you can see today was built in the 1920s by Sir James Knott. A shipbroker by trade, he established the Prince Line Limited, which was one of the largest shipping lines in the world at the turn of the

twentieth century and purchased Samares Manor in 1924. With a substantial fortune behind him, he drained the nearby salt marshes, renovated the manor house and established the beautiful gardens that you can visit today. Jersey's climate certainly lends itself to having a range of different gardens and that can be seen in the layout here with the botanical gardens. Covering 14 acres, there are numerous exotic plants in various different gardens. A water garden, rose garden, herb garden and a Japanese garden all offer wonderous sights and smells. Add to this different walks and trails amongst the trees, a number of fish and duck ponds, and there is plenty to see. Over the years, thought has also gone into catering those visitors with children as there is a labyrinth, jungle path and play area to keep all members of the family entertained. A tour of the manor house is also available for those wishing to find out more about the history and heritage of the manor, the gardens and the Knott family.

40. Seymour Tower

Built on a rocky outcrop a few miles from the south-east coast of the island in 1782, Seymour Tower was one of the 'Conway' towers that were constructed to protect Jersey from future French attack. What is different, though, is that instead of the usual round design, Seymour Tower is a square tower made from solid Jersey granite. In fact, it is the only square Conway tower on the island. It also had its main gun battery at its base as opposed to on its roof. The tower was able to command the entrance to Grouville Bay and the approach to the all-important Mont Orgueil Castle and it is known that regular signals were sent back every half hour to indicate that all was well. Like most of the Conway towers, by the mid- to late nineteenth century, Seymour Tower was abandoned in favour of the newer long-range guns, and some of these were being installed at nearby La Rocque point. At high tide, Seymour Tower looks isolated and alone way out to sea, but this part of Jersey is very deceptive. When the tide retreats, it withdraws down the shallow sloping beach and even though the tower is around a mile offshore, it is possible to walk out and explore the exterior of the tower. Caution should be advised as the tide can seemingly come in from nowhere, so do ensure to leave plenty of time! Since 2006 it has been in the hands of Jersey Heritage, who offer the opportunity for adventurous tourists to actually stay in this remote defensive tower.

Seymour Tower. (Courtesy of Dan Rok CC BY-SA 3.0)

41. Sir Winston Churchill Memorial Park

Located in St Brelade's Bay, Sir Winston Churchill Memorial Park was constructed in the 1960s in honour of Sir Winston Churchill – Britain's prime minister during the Second World War. Large wrought-iron gates mark one of the entrance ways to the park that is actually split into two sections, divided by the main road. On the beach side of the road are the formal gardens, with carefully tended to bedding areas full of vibrant plants, perfectly cut lawns, as well as a fountain, that look out over the sweeping sands of St Brelade's Bay. There are plenty of benches and

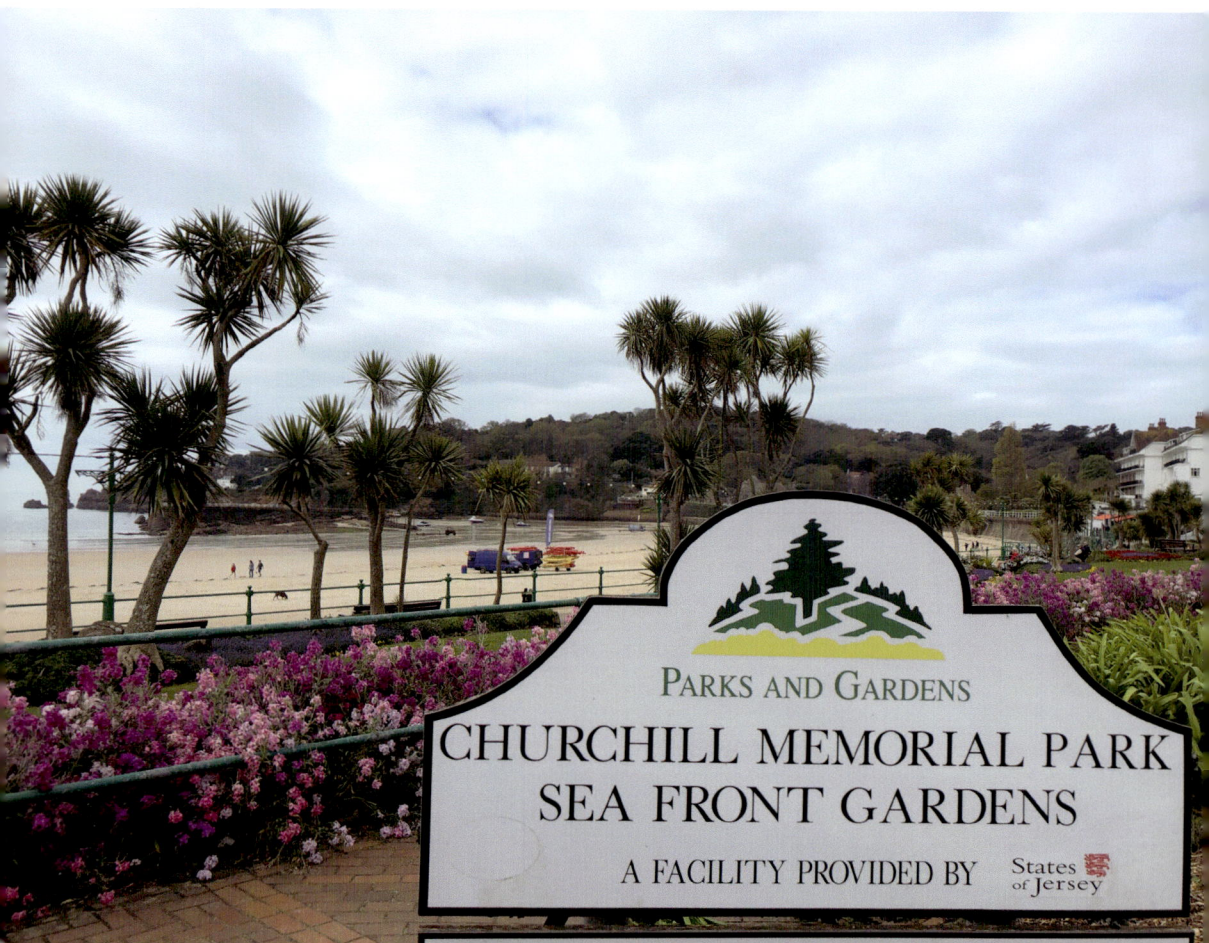

Sir Winston Churchill Memorial Park. (Author's collection)

nearby cafés and shops along the promenade to give any visitor to the area a beautiful place to sit down and simply take in the gorgeous scenery. Across the main road lies the larger part of the park, which has numerous terraces cut into the granite cliffs and is a very quiet and peaceful place. This part of the park is more left to nature, with various trees, shrubs and bushes being the perfect place for local wildlife to thrive. There is a small man-made waterfall here, along with a bust of Sir Winston Churchill that features a quote 'And our dear Channel Islands are also to be freed today' – in reference to the Channel Islands finally being liberated at the end of the Second World War. Although fairly small in the grand scheme of things, the memorial park is a quiet and free space for anyone to enjoy, whether taking a stroll and sitting down and watching the world go by and well worth a visit.

42. St Aubin's

St Aubin's Bay stretches for just over 3 miles from the capital St Helier in the east to St Aubin in the west. At high tide there is often sand still towards the middle of the bay, but at low tide the sand seemingly spreads out endlessly in all directions offering plenty of space for sunbathers, swimmers, sandcastle builders and walkers. A well-kept promenade runs the whole length too, along what was once a railway line that connected St Helier to La Corbière. The Jersey Railway operated from 1870 to 1936 (with a brief reopening by German occupying forces during the Second World War to assist with their building of fortifications on the island) and there were eight stops along St Aubin's Bay alone. The promenade is often busy with walkers, runners, cyclists and of course Le Petit Train – the land train that runs from end to end, and making the trip from one end to the other can be very rewarding for the views and the heritage.

This vast expanse of sand has a long history, linked of course to St Helier and the St Aubin fishing village. When ships unloaded their cargo at St Aubin's harbour, they were vulnerable to attack by French pirates coming into the bay. As a result, it was decided to build a tower on a rocky offshore island in the 1540s to house four guns and this was named St Aubin's Fort. During the Civil War, the Parliamentarians strengthened the site, and once the Royalists had regained control, they replaced the new earthworks with more permanent granite ramparts. The fort was redesigned in both the eighteenth and nineteenth centuries, and during the Second World War, German occupying forces strengthened the fort for their own defensive purposes by adding concrete casemates and guns. Today the fort is out of bounds to the public, but at low tide it is easily possible to walk the causeway and explore the outside of the structure.

When Hitler ordered the Channel Islands to be made into an impregnable fortress in 1941, additional bunkers and defensive positions were constructed right across Jersey and it is no surprise that this flat sandy beach, and the numerous slipways along St Aubin's Bay, received special treatment. Worried that Allied landing craft

Above: The St Aubin's Bay beach stretches around for miles! (Author's collection)

Below: Resistance Nest First Tower, clad in Jersey granite. (Author's collection)

Above: A 'dummy' bunker built into the anti-tank wall. (Author's collection)

Below: The German 'Resistance Nest Third Tower' has since been turned into the 'Gunsite Café'. (Author's collection)

might try to land here, the slipways were blocked off or destroyed, bunkers were built at regular intervals, and miles of anti-tank walls, obstacles and barbed wire were put in place. The defences stretched from Elizabeth Castle right the way round to St Aubin's harbour and the vast majority are still in situ today. Resistance Nest Millbrook is the stand-out feature along this stretch. Run by the Channel Islands Occupation Society and open at specific times of the year, it offers a glimpse into the past at what a German bunker would have been like during the occupation – and is opposite the old railway station at Millbrook. Further along, there is a false bunker built into the sea wall in an effort to confuse a potential Allied landing. One of the more unusual locations, and definitely worth a visit, is opposite an old defensive Conway tower. The Gunsite Beach Café is open all year round and is based, as you may have guessed by the name, in an old German gun emplacement! It serves a range of good quality food and is always busy. With indoor and outdoor seating, there is no better place for a hearty fried breakfast with uninterrupted views across the bay.

43. St Brelade's Bay

St Brelade's Bay is a very popular destination for tourists as it offers everything you could need in a resort and family-friendly town. Located on the south-west of the island, there are hotels, self-catering and camping facilities amongst the private

St Brelade's Bay. (Author's collection)

houses and apartments – but it wasn't always like this, with St Brelade's Bay being off the beaten track and underdeveloped until the second half of the twentieth century. Since then, however, as tourism developed, it was realised that the flat expanse of sand and sheltered waters was exactly what tourists would like! Over the years, an abundance of beach cafés, restaurants and shops have sprung up along the promenade, offering visitors everything they could possibly need. The wide golden sands of the beach provides plenty of space for everyone to find their own spot and there are a number of watersports on offer to keep people entertained, from kayaking to snorkelling. A long promenade goes along the sea wall, and for those wanting to take a break from the sun and the sea, the Sir Winston Churchill Memorial Park offers some shaded alternatives.

44. St Catherine

The St Catherine's area of Jersey in the north-east of the island is often overlooked by visitors but offers a range of different activities within a fairly short distance. St Catherine's Bay is a great place to stop and explore. It's a beach with a slightly different feel to the majority of the beaches in Jersey, with pebbles and rocks instead of soft yellow sand. There seem to be a lot of small coves joined up here on the east coast – and they are protected by a nineteenth-century built breakwater at the northern end of the bay. Original plans in the nineteenth century were for another breakwater arm to be constructed at the southern end of the beach to create a man-made harbour for the British fleet to dock, but that never materialised. A walk along the breakwater, that seems to go on forever, is a wonderful way to blow away the cobwebs. Halfway along is The Three Arches, the perfect spot to grab a drink and a snack before continuing to the end and take in the views that can stretch on for miles and miles on a clear day. It's a popular area for those looking to sail, canoe or fish.

In the middle of St Catherine's Bay is Archirondel Tower, a Conway tower that was built in 1794 to help deter a potential French attack on the beach. It was later used by German Occupying Forces in the Second World War, and today it is available as a holiday let – its distinctive red and white paint facing seawards. There are a few other German defensive bunkers in the area, a number of which are now on private land and used by the landowners.

Slightly further inland from the shore is St Catherine's Wood, a beautiful and tranquil place that is perfect for a quiet stroll or a family adventure. A circular route winds its way through the woods, with steams flowing across the paths and plenty of woodland wildlife to spot. Red squirrels can be seen scrambling up the tree trunks and plenty of birds also make the most of the woods. In amongst the trees, you might be able to find some swings and dens that have been built by previous groups, making this a lovely place to spend a few hours in the company of nature.

A view of St Catherine Bay. (Courtesy of Ian Pinion CC BY-ND 2.0)

45. St Helier

Arriving in Jersey by ferry will inevitably see you land at St Helier, and whilst most will likely be staying elsewhere on the island, the capital is well worth exploring. Over one-third of the island's population live here and it has long since been the principal town in Jersey. Named after a Belgium monk named Helerius, who landed on the nearby group of rocks named L'Islet in around AD 550, he established a small hermitage and converted Jersey's population to Christianity. He was later killed by sea-going raiders, and from this point the hermitage, which can be found just off Elizabeth Castle, became a prominent place of pilgrimage. As the harbour developed, so did the town, becoming the central point for trade and commerce.

In November 1806, work began on a defensive fortification right in the middle of St Helier on the high ground known as Town Hill or Mont de la Ville. This high ground had previously been used by local troops in 1781 during the Battle of Jersey in order to stop the invading French force from retreating from the town, and it is a little surprising that no permanent defensive structure had not been built here before seeing as it has a commanding view over the town and harbour – although it had been used as a signal station. It was the aftermath of the Battle of Jersey and the perceived weakness of Elizabeth Castle being cut off by the tide for the majority of each day, which led to a new base for the British troops being built.

Local labourers assisted the Royal Engineers over the next eight years in building a fortress that would have embrasures for an impressive one hundred cannons. Named after the Prince Regent, King George III, a 5.5-metre-thick curtain wall was built on the western and eastern flanks of a large parade ground that stretched across the top. Each flank had a large bastion and there was a large ditch on the eastern side. To aid with the stability of the buildings on top, as well as the defence of the fort, a staggering 210-metre artificial slope was constructed at the southern end, known as a glacis. As well as the bastions, Fort Regent had four redans, which allowed any cannons placed there the ability to fire on any forces attacking from any direction.

Fort Regent stood watch over St Helier for the next 150 years and held the main British garrison on the island. During the Second World War, the difficult decision was made to demilitarise the islands and the Royal Militia of the Island of Jersey left the fort on 20 June 1940. It isn't surprising that the German forces who subsequently occupied the island commandeered the fort and used it for themselves – adding flak positions to the existing structures. After the conflict, the fort was deemed to have outlived its usefulness as a military position and was used as a storage area, and later a leisure centre, which was closed in 2009.

St Helier has a lot to offer anyone visiting as it is full of history around every corner. Aside from its links to the Battle of Jersey, there is also Liberation Square – which marks the islands liberation from five years of German occupation during

Victoria Park, St Helier. (Author's collection)

One of the German gun emplacements dating from the occupation.

the Second World War. There are a number of fine museums available to visit: the Jersey Museum, the Georgian House and the Maritime Museum – all offer a good wet weather option for those days when the beaches are less attractive because of the rain, as does the shopping opportunities that are available. The ever-popular Battle of the Flowers takes place here, and the spectacular Elizabeth Castle is just a stones throw away, and there are numerous well-kept parks that provide something different to the golden sands or busy streets.

46. St Ouen's Bay

Spanning almost the entire length of the west coast of Jersey, St Ouen's Bay has 5 miles of flat golden sand and the rolling waves of the Atlantic Ocean crashing into it each day. When visiting here, it often feels a bit devoid of tourists, and perhaps it is a little bit overlooked by those who prefer the sheltered smaller beaches the island has to offer. Facing the Atlantic does mean it can get its fair share of strong winds and rough seas but that shouldn't put anyone off visiting this glorious part of Jersey – least of all surfers, who can catch plenty of waves – and the sheer size of the beach means there are other activities such as blokarting, kite and wind surfing. The beach is also perfect for those wanting to try out paragliding, with the sands providing the ideal landing zone! For those wanting to simply sunbath and take it easy, you'll have no problem in finding your own quiet part of the beach, and when the tide goes out, there are a lot of rock pools that can be explored. At various points along the main road are some stunning eateries that cater for every budget – but these can get very busy, and understandably so in the evenings, when the sunsets can be mesmerising. Then, there's the history. The nineteenth-century La Rocco Tower sits smack bang in the middle of the bay; the iconic La Corbière Lighthouse juts out at its most southernly edge and is easily visible from most parts of the beach; and like most places in Jersey, the Second World War has also left its mark. During the German occupation, such a vast open expanse of land would have been an obvious landing ground for any potential Allied liberation of the island, the occupying forces wasted no time in building a number of defences right along this beautiful stretch of Jersey. There are bunkers and pillboxes across the bay, most of which are now sealed up, but the Channel Islands Military Museum towards the northern end of St Ouen's Bay is actually housed in one of the German casemates. Whatever time of day you visit, you will be in for a feast of the senses, as there is so much to take in and it is certainly worth returning at a different time to see how the landscape changes.

A German bunker overlooking St Ouen's Bay. (Author's collection)

A view of St Ouen's Bay. (Author's collection)

47. Strongpoint Corbière

Corbière was an obvious location for German troops to build defensive positions during the occupation in the Second World War. At the southern end of the vast stretch of sand at St Ouen's Bay, and the point closest to any potential Allied shipping heading into the bay of St Malo, construction of the strongpoint took place between 1942 and 1943. It was made to 'Fortress' standard, which saw the external walls of the six fortifications built here having a thickness of an impressive 2 metres. The 2nd Company of Machine Gun Battalion 16 were stationed here, which meant a garrison of around 800–900 men saw out the duration of the war with the iconic Corbière Lighthouse always in their vision. The lighthouse was manned by the German Navy, who operated the light and a radio post from there.

At the lower end of the headland, nearest to the lighthouse, is a bunker for a 60 cm searchlight. It could find targets up to 3.5 km away and was wheeled in and out of the bunker as required. Next to it is a casemate known as K1, which had a French gun installed. The German Army had acquired a number of these from the surrender of the French in 1940 and used them in bunkers – taking them off their original wheeled carriages, for which they were no longer of any use, and mounting them onto a fixed position.

Another 10.5 cm coastal defensive casemate, known as K2, was built into the hill side to cover the approaches to Petit Port Bay and St Ouen's Bay and is one of the bunkers that has been restored and maintained by the Channel Islands Occupation Society (CIOS). There are a number of other personnel shelters, machine-gun emplacements and small rifle nests scattered right across the headland, but there are a remarkable set of bunkers in the very middle of the site that are well worth visiting.

Restored by the CIOS to its original wartime appearance, there is a Type 634 – a six-loopholed machine-gun turret bunker that was a focal point of Strongpoint Corbière. On slightly higher ground than its neighbour, there were six armoured periscopes, along with radio communications that meant observations and commands for the whole site would have been sent from here. Close by is a Type 633 M19 mortar bunker that has a staggering 40-ton steel turret! From here, 5 cm mortar bombs could be fired at a range of 875 metres, which would mean being able to hit any potential Allied attacks as they come across the rocks below. What makes these two bunkers even more impressive is the long underground passage that links them, and walking through this tunnel, followed by climbing up a ladder to get into the mortar bunker, is an experience the German troops during the Second World War would have done countless times. The inside of the CIOS-maintained bunkers are certainly thought provoking. The attention to detail and inclusion of period artefacts really does allow you to imagine what it was like to be stationed here. There are plenty of information panels, and as the bunkers are only open on certain days of the year, the volunteers are able to answer any questions you might have about the site. The small details in the living sections are especially poignant, with posters and pictures on the walls, cards on a table, a guitar lying on a bed all emphasising the point that although they were the occupier, the German troops here were still someone's father/brother/son.

The external parts of Strongpoint Corbière are accessible to view all year round, and it is easily possible to spend the whole day exploring the wider headland, with the nearby lighthouse and beautiful views.

Strongpoint Corbière during the occupation. (Courtesy of the Channel Islands Occupation Society (Jersey))

Above: A view of the strongpoint overlooking La Corbière Lighthouse. (Courtesy of the Channel Islands Occupation Society (Jersey))

Left: One of the many rooms that have been restored to how it would have looked during the occupation. (Author's collection)

Above: The long underground connecting corridor between two bunkers. (Author's collection)

Below: The original 10.5 cm gun still inside the K2 casemate bunker. (Author's collection)

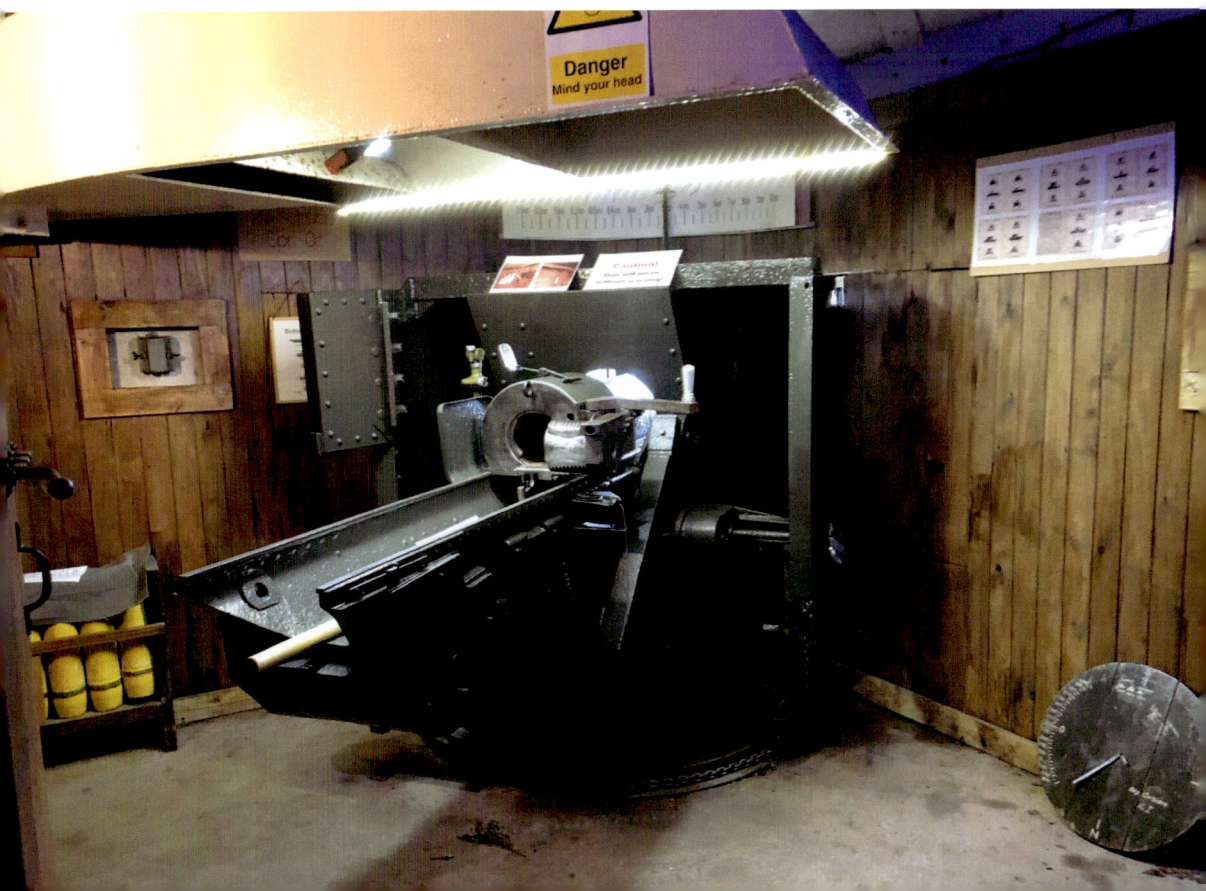

48. The Elms and Le Quétivel Mill

The National Trust of Jersey was formed in the late 1930s with the ambition of caring for and safeguarding the island's beauty and heritage. The preceding years had seen a lot of building across the island, and the trust was established in an effort to look after some not just historical buildings but also the natural environment, and today over 170 sites are under their protection.

The trust's headquarters is at The Elms, an eighteenth-century farmhouse with nearly 20 acres of land and numerous outbuildings that was bequeathed to the trust in 1975. Some of the features on site date to before this time, and although the main house and farmhouse are not open to the public, it is possible to visit the walled garden, farmyard and pressoir during the normal opening hours.

Only a few miles south of The Elms is the glorious Le Moulin de Quétivel – the only working watermill on the whole island. Records show that there has been a

watermill on this site for a staggering 700 years. Rebuilt and developed over the centuries, the current structure dates from the eighteenth century and it was a working mill right up until the twentieth century – being used briefly during the German occupation of the island in the Second Word War. Surrounded by some lovely woodland walks that are able to be explored, as well as a pond and a herb garden, there is an Open Milling Day every year where members of the public are able to come and see the mill in action grinding wheat into flour.

49. The Georgian House Museum

Located at No. 16 New Street in St Helier, the National Trust of Jersey have renovated this old Georgian house, which was built in the early eighteenth century, into a rather impressive museum. Situated in the middle of St Helier, the townhouse is spread over three floors and has been furnished to represent what it would have looked like at some point at the beginning of the nineteenth century. At this time, the Journeaux family were residing in the property, and a film in one of the rooms tells you about this well-to-do family. Downstairs in the Georgian kitchen, a volunteer

The front of the restored Georgian House. (Courtesy of Gary Grimshaw/NTJ)

dressed as the housekeeper is on hand to explain what food was like at the time, with the opportunity to even try some! To keep the children entertained, there is a Glorious Georgian Activity Sheet, with plenty of things for them to spot and do on the way round, which makes this museum well worth putting on your itinerary – especially if the weather scuppers any outdoor plans.

50. The Radio Tower

The Radio Tower is situated on the same headland as Strongpoint Corbière and Corbière Lighthouse and was built during the Second World War by German occupying forces. With Hitler's plans to turn Jersey into a fortress, a number of large coastal batteries were planned and built across the island. These positions would not only defend the island from potential Allied attack but could also be used to strike

The Radio Tower has views that stretch on for miles. (Author's collection)

at any Allied shipping that passed to close to the Channel Islands of the Cotentin peninsula. To do this effectively, they also planned to construct eight Naval Direction and Range-Finding Towers across Jersey to coordinate, control and direct the battery fire accurately. Known as Marinepeilstäden unde Maßstellen *in* German, only three were actually built, with this being MP2. With walls around 2 metres thick and standing nearly 18 metres high, MP2 had a stunning view of this part of the Jersey coastline. During the war it was disguised as one of Jersey's granite-built Conway towers and when the conflict was over, it came under the control of the States of Jersey Harbours and Airport Committee, who installed a 360-degree glass control room. In 2006, Jersey Heritage became the custodians of the site and they have renovated the inside, whilst keeping original features, to turn the tower into a self-catering holiday let. The bedrooms are simple and effective, but it is all about location. The top glass covered floor has been turned into the most spectacular dining and sitting room, with incredible views of everything all around. With Corbière Lighthouse in one direction and the lights of Elizabeth Castle and St Helier in the other, it offers a panorama of Jersey like no other.

Acknowledgements

What a fascinating book this has been to research. I have been fortunate enough to have visited Jersey a number of times in my life, and each time I have discovered more idyllic locations and incredible places of history, making me want to return again and again. It has been an exhilarating and time-consuming process, as I've been able to rediscover locations, buildings and ruins, in addition to uncovering new sights, sounds and stories. Jersey has so much to offer and choosing just fifty places of interest was a fraught process! It has been a delight to be able to explore this wonderful place with my own family in tow, and just seeing the excitement on my children's faces as a vast castle comes into view, or hearing the thrill in their voice as they scuttle across a near deserted beach, reminds me of just how captivating Jersey can be.

In this day and age it is possible to do a lot of research online and with books, but nothing compares to actually heading out and exploring things for yourself. Only then, when you see these stunning locations in their original environment, and you are able to talk to those who work and live there every day, does it start to make sense and your writing can take shape. This book hasn't been without its challenges though. Condensing the illustrious history of a centuries old castle into just a few hundred words is a hard thing to do. Investigating the different aspects of this book has led me to find out some incredible things and meet a number of wonderful people, all of whom have been willing to share their knowledge and expertise, and this is so important in passing on the history of our communities to the next generation.

I need to express my gratitude to the many organisations, people and photographers who have kindly shared their knowledge and allowed me to use their photographic work in my book, with a special mention to Dave Sewell for his local help and advice; Nicola de Louche at Le Petit Train (www.littletrain.co.uk); Damien Horn from the Channel Islands Military Museum (www.facebook.com/The-Channel-Island-Military-Museum); all at Visit Jersey for their support (www.jersey.com) and Donna Le Marrec and everyone at National Trust Jersey for their help and guidance with my research (www.nationaltrust.je).

A huge thank you needs to go to everyone at the Channel Islands Occupation Society (CIOS) for their warmth, knowledge and enthusiasm – in particular to Daniel Clark, Elaine Curtis and Malcolm Amy (www.facebook.com/ciosjersey). Their passion for preserving the history and heritage of the island during the German occupation of the Second World War is simply incredible and their hard work, all voluntary, ensures that the island's story continues to be told.

There also needs to be a mention for everyone at Jersey Heritage, especially Hilary Grimes, Val Nelson and Helena Kergozou, who have been so helpful and accommodating across all their sites, as well as being willing to share their expertise and access to their photographic archives with me (www.jerseyheritage.org). Jersey Heritage oversee a large number of the most iconic sites on the island, with members of staff at each location being vastly knowledgeable and always happy to share information and answer every question.

I would also like to thank Nick Grant, Nikki Embery, Jenny Bennett and all at Amberley Publishing for their help in making this project become a reality, as well as my wife Laura and sons James and Ryan, who accompanied me on some wonderful trips to this beautiful island, and who can't wait to return and explore again.

About the Author

Andrew Powell-Thomas writes military history, local heritage and children's fiction books. He regularly speaks at events, libraries, schools and literary festivals, as well as making appearances on television and radio. It is possible to keep up with everything he is up to by following him on social media or by visiting his website at www.andrewpowell-thomas.co.uk.

Andrew's other titles available with Amberley Publishing:

Castles of Scotland
The West Country's Last Line of Defence: Taunton Stop Line
Historic England: Somerset
50 Gems of Somerset
50 Gems of Wiltshire
50 Gems of the Isle of Wight
Cornwall's Military Heritage
Devon's Military Heritage
Somerset's Military Heritage
Wiltshire's Military Heritage
The Channel Islands' Military Heritage
The Isle of Wight's Military Heritage
Castles and Fortifications of the West Country